THRIVING GOOD LIFE

Thoughtful gifts for the ones you love

Visit our website: thrivinggoodlife.com

IN MY
MOTHER'S
WORDS

THE MEMORIES & STORIES
OF HER LIFE

CONTENT

From Me to You   1

Vital Statistics   2

Your Family Tree   4

You & Your Parents   6

Your Memories of Growing Up   16

Family Traditions & Stories   44

Your School Years   56

Your Adult Years   66

Your Life As A Mother   82

A Few of Your Favourite Things   94

FROM ME TO YOU

Dear _____

How lovely it would be to learn more about your life.

What it was like growing up when you did. The stories from your childhood, your family, and the memories you hold dear.

So here's a special gift we can both enjoy. A journal with space for you to tell your stories, share your experiences, hopes and dreams, and impart advice.

I'd love for you to fill this in. You can start wherever you like, either working through the prompts in sequence, or at random. Once complete, I'd love you to hand it back to me so I can share your memories with future generations of our family.

We can even complete this journal together, if you'd like. With me asking you questions and recording your responses within the pages of this book.

There may be questions or prompts you don't want to answer, and that's OK. I know whatever you choose to share will be meaningful.

Think of this as our little keepsake. Something to treasure.

I'm excited to learn more about you.

With all my love.

From _____

VITAL STATISTICS

YOUR FULL BIRTH NAME IS:

DATE OF BIRTH:

PLACE OF BIRTH:

EYE COLOUR:

HAIR COLOUR:

BLOOD TYPE:

MAJOR OPERATIONS:

MEDICAL CONDITIONS:

OTHER INFORMATION:

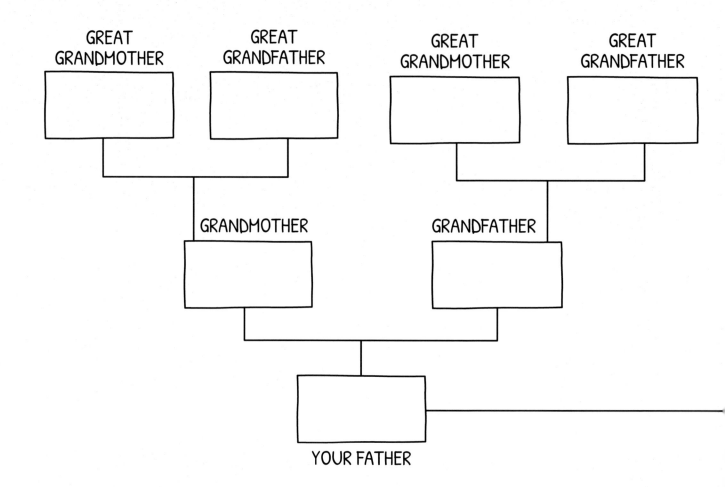

GREAT GRANDMOTHER

GREAT GRANDFATHER

GREAT GRANDMOTHER

GREAT GRANDFATHER

GRANDMOTHER

GRANDFATHER

YOUR FATHER

YOUR FAMILY TREE

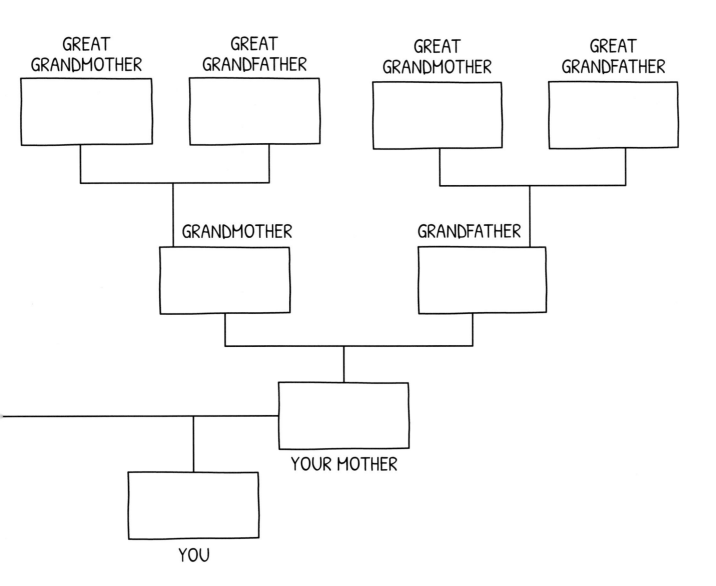

GREAT GRANDMOTHER

GREAT GRANDFATHER

GREAT GRANDMOTHER

GREAT GRANDFATHER

GRANDMOTHER

GRANDFATHER

YOUR MOTHER

YOU

YOU & YOUR PARENTS

WHEN AND WHERE WAS YOUR MOTHER BORN?

WHEN AND WHERE WAS YOUR FATHER BORN?

HOW DID THEY MEET?

WHAT DID YOUR MOTHER DO FOR WORK?

WHAT DID YOUR FATHER DO FOR WORK?

WHICH OF YOUR PARENTS DO YOU LOOK LIKE THE MOST?

WHICH OF THEIR CHARACTER TRAITS DO YOU POSSESS?

WHAT FUNNY FUNNY HABITS OR SAYINGS DID THEY HAVE?

WHAT WAS THEIR FAVOURITE THING TO DO ON THE WEEKEND?

HOW MANY SIBLINGS DID YOUR PARENTS HAVE? WHAT ARE THEIR NAMES?

WHAT STORY FROM YOUR CHILDHOOD DO YOUR PARENTS OFTEN BRING UP?

THE MOST IMPORTANT LESSON(S) YOU LEARNED FROM YOUR PARENTS

WHAT ADVICE DO YOU STILL FOLLOW TO THIS DAY?

HOW WOULD YOU DESCRIBE YOUR RELATIONSHIP WITH YOUR PARENTS?

WHAT DO YOU WISH THEY DID MORE OF?

WHAT DO YOU WISH YOU DID MORE OF?

WHAT RULES DID YOUR PARENTS SET FOR YOU AS A TEENAGER?

WHICH RULE DID YOU REBEL AGAINST THE MOST?

WHAT'S THE MOST SURPRISING THING ABOUT YOUR PARENTS?

GROWING UP, WHO WAS THE MOST EMBARRASSING PARENT? EXPLAIN WHY.

WHAT DID YOU MOST ADMIRE AND APPRECIATE ABOUT YOUR PARENTS?

WHAT ELSE WOULD YOU LIKE TO TELL ME ABOUT MY GRANDPARENTS?

YOUR MEMORIES OF GROWING UP

WHAT WAS LIFE LIKE GROWING UP DURING THE TIMES YOU DID?

WHAT WAS YOUR HOME LIKE? HOW MANY ROOMS WERE THERE? WHAT AMENITIES DID YOU HAVE? HOW WAS YOUR HOME DIFFERENT TO THE HOME YOU HAVE TODAY?

DESCRIBE THE NEIGHBOURHOOD YOU GREW UP IN

HOW OFTEN DID YOU PLAY OUTSIDE? WHAT GAMES DID YOU PLAY?

WAS THERE ANYTHING THAT MADE YOUR FAMILY STANDOUT FROM THE OTHER FAMILIES IN THE NEIGHBOURHOOD? WHAT WAS IT?

TELL ME ABOUT YOUR BROTHERS & SISTERS. IF YOU DIDN'T HAVE ANY SIBLINGS DESCRIBE WHAT IT WAS LIKE GROWING UP AS AN ONLY CHILD.

DID YOU HAVE A NICKNAME? WHAT WAS IT? WHO CHOSE IT, AND WHY?

DESCRIBE YOUR BEDROOM? DID YOU HAVE TO SHARE IT WITH A SIBLING? WHAT WAS THAT LIKE?

DESCRIBE A TYPICAL FAMILY MEALTIME. WHO COOKED? WHO WASHED UP?

WHAT SOUNDS OR SMELLS REMIND YOU OF CHILDHOOD?

WHAT WAS YOUR FAVOURITE WAY TO SPEND THE WEEKEND?

WHAT WERE YOU CURIOUS ABOUT WHEN YOU WERE LITTLE?

WHAT WAS THE MOST MISCHIEVOUS THING YOU EVER DID AS A CHILD?

WHAT WAS THE WORST ACCIDENT YOU EVER HAD AS A CHILD?

WHAT WERE YOU MOST PASSIONATE ABOUT OR OBSESSED WITH?

WHAT DID YOU WANT TO BE WHEN YOU GREW UP?

WHAT COMPETITIONS, TROPHIES AWARDS DID YOU WIN AS A CHILD?

WHAT WAS THE BEST GIFT YOU EVER RECEIVED?

HOW WOULD YOU DESCRIBE YOUR PERSONALITY AS A CHILD?

HOW WOULD YOUR PARENTS DESCRIBE YOUR PERSONALITY AS A CHILD?

DID YOU HAVE ANY PETS? IF SO WHAT WERE THEIR NAMES?

WHAT WAS YOUR FAVOURITE INDOOR GAME OR ACTIVITY?
WHO DID YOU PLAY IT WITH? WHO TAUGHT YOU HOW TO PLAY IT?

WHICH OF YOUR SIBLINGS WERE YOU THE CLOSEST TO? DESCRIBE YOUR RELATIONSHIP?

HOW OFTEN DID YOU SPEND TIME WITH EXTENDED FAMILY LIKE COUSINS?

WHAT'S YOUR FAVOURITE MEMORY OF VISITING YOUR GRANDPARENTS HOUSE?

WHO WAS YOUR FAVOURITE RELATIVE OUTSIDE YOUR IMMEDIATE FAMILY? WHAT SORT OF RELATIONSHIP DID YOU HAVE?

WHAT WAS YOUR FAVOURITE HOBBY?

WHAT IS YOUR HAPPIEST CHILDHOOD MEMORY?

TELL ME A FUNNY STORY FROM YOUR CHILDHOOD.

WHAT CHORES DID YOU HAVE TO DO?

_____
_____
_____
_____
_____
_____
_____
_____
_____
_____

WHAT WAS THE MOST TECHNICALLY ADVANCED ITEM
IN YOUR HOUSEHOLD?

_____
_____
_____
_____
_____
_____
_____

WHAT TIME DID YOU HAVE TO GO TO BED? HOW DID YOU FEEL ABOUT BEDTIMES?

HOW DID YOU FEEL ABOUT GETTING UP IN THE MORNINGS?

WHAT CARTOONS AND/OR TV SHOWS DID YOU WATCH AS A CHILD?

WHAT TV SHOWS WERE YOU NOT ALLOWED TO WATCH?
DID YOU EVER WATCH THEM IN SECRET?

DESCRIBE A TIME YOU GOT CAUGHT DOING SOMETHING NAUGHTY.

WHAT WAS THE WORST PUNISHMENT YOU'VE EVER RECEIVED?

WHAT WAS YOUR WEEKLY ALLOWANCE? WHAT DID YOU TYPICALLY SPEND IT ON?

DO YOU REMEMBER THE VERY FIRST THING YOU EVER BOUGHT?

TELL ME ABOUT YOUR MOST MEMORABLE FAMILY VACATION.

AT WHAT AGE WERE YOU ALLOWED TO GO PLACES BY YOURSELF? WHAT WAS THE FIRST PLACE YOU VISITED ON YOUR OWN?

WHAT TYPES OF TOYS DID YOU PLAY WITH? WHAT WAS YOUR FAVOURITE?

WHAT WAS YOUR FAVOURITE CHILDHOOD CANDY?

DESCRIBE YOUR EXPERIENCE OF LEARNING HOW TO RIDE A BICYCLE.

WHEN DID YOU LEARN HOW TO SWIM? DESCRIBE THE EXPERIENCE.

WHAT TEEN SLANG (WORDS, TERMS OR PHRASES) DID YOU AND YOUR PEERS USE?

WHAT HAIRSTYLES, CLOTHES, DANCE MOVES, SONGS WERE MOST POPULAR?

THE THING YOU MISS MOST ABOUT BEING A KID AND/OR TEEN IS...

WHAT ELSE WOULD YOU LIKE ME TO KNOW ABOUT YOUR LIFE GROWING UP?

FAMILY TRADITIONS & STORIES

SHARE AN INTERESTING FACT OR STORY ABOUT YOUR GRANDPARENTS?

WHO'S THE MOST FAMOUS OR INFAMOUS MEMBER OF YOUR FAMILY? SHARE A STORY ABOUT HIM OR HER.

NAME SOMETHING THAT'S BEEN IN YOUR FAMILY FOR GENERATIONS?

DID YOUR FAMILY HAVE ANY TRADITIONS FOR SPECIAL HOLIDAY'S LIKE CHRISTMAS OR EASTER? WHAT WERE THEY?

HOW DID YOUR FAMILY CELEBRATE OCCASIONS LIKE BIRTHDAYS AND ANNIVERSARIES?

DID YOU HAVE A RELIGIOUS UPBRINGING? DESCRIBE YOUR PLACE OF WORSHIP?

WHAT DID A TYPICAL SUNDAY LOOK LIKE IN YOUR HOUSE?

WHAT DO YOU KNOW ABOUT THE ORIGIN OF YOUR FAMILY NAME (LAST NAME)?

ARE THERE ANY TRADITIONAL NAMES OR NICKNAMES IN THE FAMILY? LIST THEM BELOW.

ARE YOU AWARE OF ANY TRADITIONAL NAMING CEREMONIES IN THE FAMILY?

HAS YOUR FAMILY ALWAYS LIVED IN THIS COUNTRY? IF NOT, WHERE DID THEY ORIGINATE FROM?

HOW AND WHY DID THEY CHOOSE TO SETTLE HERE?
WHO DID THEY HAVE TO LEAVE BEHIND?

HOW MANY LANGUAGES DO YOU SPEAK? WHAT WAS YOUR FIRST LANGUAGE?
IN WHICH SITUATIONS DO YOU SPEAK IT?

TELL ME ABOUT YOUR FAMILY'S EXPERIENCE OF SETTLING IN A NEW COUNTRY. WHAT WERE THEIR FIRST IMPRESSIONS? WHAT KIND OF WORK DID THEY DO?

SHARE A RECIPE THAT'S BEEN IN YOUR FAMILY FOR GENERATIONS

WHAT FAMILY SUPERSTITIONS OR BELIEFS DO YOU UPHOLD?

WHAT ELSE WOULD YOU LIKE ME TO KNOW ABOUT YOUR FAMILY TRADITIONS?

YOUR SCHOOL YEARS

WHAT WAS YOUR EARLIEST MEMORY OF GOING TO SCHOOL?

WHAT WAS THE NAME OF YOUR BEST FRIEND? HOW DID YOU MEET?

WHAT DID YOU LIKE ABOUT YOUR BEST FRIEND?

WHAT WERE YOU KNOWN FOR IN SCHOOL? WERE YOU A PART OF A CLIQUE?

TELL ME ABOUT A TIME WHEN YOU FELT PRESSURED TO DO SOMETHING BY YOUR PEERS? HOW DID YOU MANAGE THE SITUATION?

WHAT DID YOU LIKE/DISLIKE ABOUT GOING TO SCHOOL?

DESCRIBE THE MODE OF TRANSPORT YOU USED FOR SCHOOL.

WHICH SUBJECTS DID YOU LIKE/DISLIKE THE MOST?

WHAT SPORTS DID YOU PLAY? WHAT WAS YOUR FAVOURITE?

WHAT EXTRACURRICULAR ACTIVITIES WERE YOU INVOLVED IN?

WHAT SORT OF STUDENT WERE YOU? WHAT WERE YOUR GRADES LIKE?

WHAT DO YOU WISH THEY'D TAUGHT IN SCHOOL?

WHO WAS YOUR FAVOURITE TEACHER? WHAT IMPACT DID S/HE HAVE ON YOU?

WHAT WERE YOUR VIEWS ON HIGHER EDUCATION? DID YOU GO TO COLLEGE OR UNIVERSITY, IF SO, WHERE?

WHAT DID YOU STUDY AT COLLEGE/UNIVERSITY? WHY THAT SUBJECT?

TELL ME ABOUT WHAT COLLEGE/UNIVERSITY LIFE WAS LIKE FOR YOU?

HOW HAS DECIDING TO GO/NOT GO TO COLLEGE/UNIVERSITY IMPACTED YOUR LIFE?

WHAT ELSE WOULD YOU LIKE ME TO KNOW ABOUT YOUR SCHOOL YEARS?

YOUR ADULT YEARS

WHEN DID YOU KNOW YOU WERE NO LONGER A CHILD?

HOW OLD WERE YOU WHEN YOU FIRST LEFT HOME? WHAT WAS IT LIKE LIVING WITHOUT YOUR PARENTS?

WHAT WAS YOUR FIRST PLACE LIKE? WHY DID YOU CHOOSE TO LIVE THERE?

WHAT WAS YOUR FIRST JOB? WHAT WAS IT LIKE, AND HOW MUCH DID YOU GET PAID?

WHAT WAS THE WORST JOB YOU'VE EVER HAD?

WHAT WAS THE BEST JOB YOU'VE EVER HAD?

WHAT WAS THE TOUGHEST CHALLENGE YOU'VE HAD TO FACE IN THE WORKPLACE?

WHAT'S THE MOST VALUABLE LESSON YOU'VE LEARNED ABOUT MONEY?

DESCRIBE ONE THING YOU BOUGHT THAT WAS CONSIDERED A LUXURY AT THE TIME.

WHAT'S ONE THING YOU'VE ALWAYS WANTED TO DO BUT HAVEN'T?

WHAT'S THE HARDEST OR MOST STRESSFUL THING ABOUT ADULTHOOD?

AT WHAT STAGE IN LIFE DID YOU FEEL YOUR MOST CONFIDENT?

WHO WAS THE LOVE OF YOUR LIFE? WHEN, WHERE AND HOW DID YOU MEET?

DESCRIBE YOUR FIRST DATE - WHERE DID YOU GO? WHAT DID YOU WEAR?

TELL ME ABOUT YOUR FIRST KISS?

WHAT WAS DATING LIKE FOR YOU WHEN YOU WERE YOUNGER?

WHAT'S YOUR BEST ADVICE WHEN IT COMES TO FALLING IN LOVE?

WHAT ADVICE WOULD YOU GIVE TO YOUR 20-YEAR OLD SELF?

ARE YOU STILL FRIENDS WITH ANYONE FROM YOUR CHILDHOOD? WHO? WHY DO YOU THINK YOU'RE STILL FRIENDS AFTER ALL THIS TIME?

WHAT'S YOUR BEST ADVICE WHEN IT COMES TO CHOOSING FRIENDS?

COMPARED TO WHEN YOU WERE A CHILD IS LIFE SIMPLER OR MORE COMPLICATED?

WHAT DO YOU THINK LIFE WILL BE LIKE FOR THE NEXT GENERATION?

OUT OF ALL THE BIRTHDAY'S YOU'VE HAD, WHICH HAVE YOU LOOKED FORWARD TO THE MOST? WHICH BIRTHDAY HAVE YOU DREADED (OR DREAD). WHY?

WHAT'S BEEN THE GREATEST TECHNOLOGICAL ADVANCEMENT OF YOUR TIME?

WHICH PERSON (ALIVE OR DEAD) HAS BEEN YOUR GREATEST INFLUENCE?

WHAT'S THE MOST SIGNIFICANT NEWS EVENT THAT'S HAPPENED DURING YOUR LIFETIME? WHAT IMPACT DID IT HAVE ON YOU AND THE WORLD AT LARGE?

WHAT ARE YOU MOST THANKFUL FOR IN LIFE?

WHAT ARE YOUR GOALS FOR THE FUTURE?

WHAT DO YOU WANT TO LEAVE AS YOUR LEGACY?

WHAT ELSE WOULD YOU LIKE ME TO KNOW ABOUT
YOUR EXPERIENCE OF ADULTHOOD?

YOUR LIFE AS A MOTHER

DESCRIBE HOW YOU FELT WHEN YOU DISCOVERED YOU WERE PREGNANT?

WHAT WAS IT LIKE CARRYING ME IN YOUR WOMB?

WHAT DID YOU LOVE ABOUT BEING PREGNANT? WHAT DIDN'T YOU LOVE?

DID YOU HAVE ANY CRAVINGS WHILE PREGNANT? WHAT WERE THEY?

WHAT DO YOU REMEMBER ABOUT MY BIRTH?

WHAT DO YOU REMEMBER ABOUT THE FIRST TIME YOU HELD ME?

WHAT DOES MY NAME MEAN? WHO CHOSE IT?

WHAT WERE THE OTHER NAMES ON THE LIST?

IF I WAS BORN A DIFFERENT SEX, WHAT WOULD YOU HAVE NAMED ME?

WHAT ARE YOUR MOST MEMORABLE 'FIRST' MOMENTS WITH ME?

WHAT SURPRISED YOU THE MOST ABOUT BECOMING A MOTHER?

IN WHAT WAYS HAS THE EXPERIENCE CHANGED YOU?

WHAT'S BEEN YOUR MOST REWARDING MOMENT AS A MOTHER?

DESCRIBE YOUR SCARIEST MOMENT AS A MOTHER.

WHAT'S BEEN YOUR PROUDEST MUM MOMENT?

WHAT'S BEEN THE MOST CHALLENGING THING ABOUT RAISING CHILDREN?

IN WHAT WAYS ARE WE ALIKE/NOT ALIKE?

AT WHAT POINT DID YOU REALISE I WASN'T A LITTLE KID ANYMORE?
HOW DID YOU ADJUST TO THAT?

WHAT ARE YOUR DREAMS AND HOPES FOR YOUR CHILDREN'S FUTURE?

IF YOU COULD BECOME A MUM ALL OVER AGAIN, WHAT WOULD YOU DO DIFFERENTLY?

WHAT ELSE WOULD YOU LIKE ME TO KNOW ABOUT YOU AS A MOTHER?

A FEW OF YOUR FAVOURITE THINGS

TIME OF YEAR

PLACE TO TAKE A VACATION

POEM AND/OR SONG

BOOK AND/OR AUTHOR

QUOTE

FAVOURITE THING TO DO WHEN ALONE

RESTAURANT

ICE-CREAM

DRINK

FOOD

DESSERT

ANIMAL

COLOUR

SCENT OR PERFUME

FLOWERS/PLANTS

ACTOR/ACTRESS

ARTIST

INSTRUMENT

MOVIE

SPORT

WHAT ELSE WOULD YOU LIKE TO SHARE WITH ME?

Made in United States
North Haven, CT
24 January 2024

47780725R00057